No Whiskey,
No Tears

Also by Stephen Sharpe:

Defining Love

Afterword Press

ISBN: 978-1-952555-02-2

No Whiskey, No Tears

A Collection of Poems

By

Stephen Sharpe

Dedicated to

Silvia,
My amazing wife, best friend, heartbeat, and muse

My future child(ren),
May you learn from my decisions and distractions.

Table of Contents

Stumbling Through the Night

"...a story from my travels."

Hobo Manifesto

Who am I to ask for your money?
I don't know what you had to do get it,
Or what you plan to spend it on.
And you don't know what I'd do with it.

Think of it as a small investment in another life,
Another story,
Another memory.
Believe me, it will always pay off.

Your contribution will help me get through the day.
If possible, I'll earn it through any help that I can provide,
Or with a story from my travels.
That way, we'll both end up having a better day.

Funeral for a Flower

I found a smashed flower on the sidewalk today.
I couldn't tell what kind it was or where it came from.
Mutilated beyond recognition,
With only a leaf and a withered petal left.

I wonder if it broke through the concrete, only to be stomped on by someone in a rush.
Maybe it was carelessly plucked, only to be tossed away after the occasion.
I hope that it didn't go through the agony of being grown and cared for,
Only to be destroyed in a fit of love me nots.
I hope it still lives on in someone's happy memories
And that it was told at least once that it was beautiful.

Black Tie Affair

Funerals are for the living.
Weddings are for the dead.
Both are to give closure.

One is for the celebration of a life lived,
The other is for relationships that died in order to make this union possible.
With all dressed to impress and to show respect for the occasion,
Tears of sorrow and joy lead to appreciation of what you have and hope for.

All lips kiss of best wishes and fond memories,
So no ill will is spoken.
Words too often a long time coming are finally raised and closure is finally found,
Until death becomes that great divide.

Late for the Party

Laughter,
Commotion, and indistinguishable conversations
Slowly trickle from upstairs.

Smiles going up,
Smiles coming down,
With a few frowns and dazed looks to break up the monotony.

Stragglers and outcasts become self-designated hall monitors.
A few stop to ask for directions, while some eyes ask for guidance.
They all feel bad for each other,
The ones that stayed too long
And those late for the party.

Fine as Wine

Regardless of the tone of our skin,
They pull us all down by the grapevine.
Money is made off of the bodies that they walked all over,
Trying to put our seeds in the ground,
Leaving us with buried feelings.
But they say that we're supposed to get better with time,
Supposed to get put on a pedestal.
I'm waiting for our people to get a taste of excellence.

Who Comforts the Strong?

For the ones that they
Often turn to for their strength,
Who is there for them?

Epitome

Since I see her as a fixture like me, I never took the time to approach her.
Even at her sexiest, I never say more than "hope you enjoyed yourself and
thanks for the support."
I haven't made a move because she needs a friend more than a lover.
Plus, I've seen how she does guys, and I don't do well with rejection.
So I have the thankless job of every week trying to discourage the new guys,
saying, "I wouldn't if I were you…"
But words go unheeded as they get bruised egos and hurt feelings,
Possibly pockets too if she was feeling thirsty that night.

To most, she seems cold and distant, when she's just trying to put space
between her and the past that has left her numb.
Yet she'll bite her lip and turn away around sensitive subjects because
though wounds heal, the pain always runs deep when that nerve is hit.
Since tears never flow upward,
They're easily missed by those that look at her from the bottom up.

She doesn't know that she's one of the reasons that I keep writing about love.
An epitome of my poetry,
Yes, I know in the pit of me that she too was a victim of Cupid's bad aim,
Incompetent at his job and not likely to compensate us for his mistakes.
I wanted to show her that I'm only here to help and that I care.
I just want her to be able to say that Stephen Sharpe cared,
But I could tell that her mind condensed it to S.S. cared.
Just like her, I don't think you got that, summed up as s-scared that I'm like
every other guy.
It'd be hard to quickly prove otherwise because the only thing that
differentiates us is a combination of situations, nature, and nurture.
But it's in my nature to nurture those going through tough situations,
Especially ones bottled up under the pressure of judgment.
Not wanting flaws to show, people try to smooth them and divert attention,
Which usually works since most never look past the shell to find a person's
true value.
She's interesting at first glance but holds so much more if you take the time.

I was told that life is in the details, so I notice the little things.
I noticed how she's not a flashy dresser, yet she wears big bracelets.
I wonder if it's to hide scars or make it harder to get a good grip on her wrist.
I've watched too many guys make the mistake of reaching for her hand
Or even worse, coming from behind and trying to whisper in her ear.

9

She flinches every time because that voice can belong to anyone, hot breath gives a clue to its owner's true form but reverts to something more human once they're face to face.

Though most are left denied, on those lonely nights she might concede, Putting in a little extra work to make herself stand out in a crowd.

They're all trying to do the same and though she might accomplish her goal, she's never singled out.

Many of those calling aren't that picky, so she's bachelorette #4, But she still smiles after a rough day when they tell her how beautiful she is, night in and night out.

What she doesn't know is that I singled her out, dedicating this night to getting to know her.

Even though she's beautiful to me, I'll ask if she considers herself that way.

Trying to find her place as a rose among thorns, it's no wonder that butterflies are drawn to her.

Some do short flybys, while others decide to make their nest inside her Causing that crawling feeling along her skin, while she's thinking, 'no, no, not again.'

Not wanting to be hurt again by amateur gardeners and caterpillars That slowly chip away at the pillars of self-worth, love, happiness, and trust that she tries so carefully to maintain.

She knows that once a rose loses its look, its thrown away without a thought, And her petals have slowly been plucked by love me and love me nots.

So she tries to hold her petals together with tapered dresses and thorns.

The same thorns keeping most people further than arms' reach, Scared of being pricked, not realizing that the thickest ends are sticking her.

Yet she still smiles whenever I see her, just enjoying some poetry and being out in the fresh air.

Never knowing where the night will lead, who knows if she might find that bachelor #19 is a gardener, who is more like a guardian.

Someone who can encase her in a vase to catch her tears of insecurity, let it mix into her roots,

And surround her with baby's breath to bring back that innocent hope of a better tomorrow.

All just to help her bloom in peace, in her own time, and simply make her smile in the meantime,

Knowing that someone took the time to notice little details, not caring about flaws,

And used fragile fragments of broken hearts to show why there'll always be a need for gentle men.

Self Portrait

I once read that every portrait that's painted with feeling is a portrait of the
artist, and not the sitter.
That makes most art autobiographical if you think about all things
considered.
That means that all of my writing has really just been portraits of me,
Of how I see the world, or how I wish that it could be.

Each poem adds a piece to the collage of my life,
So I don't have to say much, since my ink blots will suffice.
One who hates being misconstrued
Can take the time to carefully spell out what is true,
Write, delete, hide, reveal, revel,
Explore exactly what stories to tell
And how they should be told,
Leaving passages to secrets that mental blocks might hold.
Pieces of a puzzle waiting to be put together and mysteries left to find,
All leading you to get a genuine look of what goes on inside my mind.

Translation

They say it's all in the presentation,
But what happens when things get lost in translation?
Added lines and page breaks that I didn't authorize.
Punctuations and words split by a translator into an almost unreadable
language.

Messages skewed between mediums.
What I write in pencil hides the second guessing that shows in the scratches
of a pen.
What I write in Word loses the fading of ink and lead that reminds me of
how long I've been doing this.
What I write in note applications forfeits the ability to retrace my steps and
undo mistakes.

Written or spoken,
Read or heard,
Passions are transcribed into cords,
Hopefully connected to open receivers.

Breaking Up the Band

"Either them or me."
She gave the ultimatum.
My friends and I laughed.

Cut Down To Size

This is dedicated to all the good guys and bad bees, especially Ms. Take,
Because I always seemed to give and all she ever did was take,
So she'll forever remember her mistake of crossing this poet.
If I'm cupid on the mic then she must be stupid in the dress that's too tight,
Cutting off the circulation to the brain
Because she must be an airhead to think it'd be ok to try to get over on a
good guy.

Obviously, you have me confused with someone else
Because I am not the one to be taken lightly or to assume that I'd be fine just
playing a role.
So allow me to reintroduce myself, my name is Stephen spelt with a pH.
Indicators show that my current level is strongly acidic like the juices
churning in your stomach,
As you realize that the butterflies are melting and that there is no love in this
poem.
But don't think that I've forgotten where my roots are based, I'm just leaving
my mark like bleach on your favorite outfit.
It wouldn't faze you as much if you were really as sparkly white and spotless
as you want people to believe.
If you thought that it'd get past me, you must have forgotten that my last
name is Sharpe.
And yes all of the puns do apply, from the way that I dress to my intellect.
I finished high school by 16, received two degrees before I could legally
drink,
And my life is far from dull, internationally known from Peru to Chile,
Argentina, Mexico, Brazil and some parts of Europe.
You don't have to tell me I'm legit because I have a big ego that's reinforced
everyday by the people who address me as Mr. Sharpe on the job.
Obviously, my game is on point, so handle me with care.
If you do, it can be all good and I'll cut you like the Scorpio I am.
But if not, I might have to cut you down to size.
When I say I'm sharp, I mean precise, so I cut out all of the unnecessary
drama in my life.
Like the saying goes, "Behind every good man is a few women left in the
dust."

Because too often women talk a good game, but when they really meet a
good man they freeze up, run away, or start sabotaging themselves.
I don't have time for all of that, so I keep it moving towards my goals.

I know that you're probably turned off by my realness, just like I am by your fakeness.
So I wonder what's fake about you tonight...is it your hair color or your hair itself?
Your eyelashes, eye color, or is it something under your skin...like your personality?
Yet you claim that you always keep it 100.
I bet that the only thing that is real about you are your tears,
And I couldn't care less if they're for me or you.
I know that sounds heartless, but no one cries for a heartbreaker.
Though it's heartbreakingly pitiful that you can't keep a single man, so you settle for some attention and pieces of a few men at a distance, kept at bay by your looks and reputation,
Scared to let them in to see the real you because they might leave when they see what I do.

You see, before I even asked for your number my trick-sense was tingling,
But I was curious so I gave you the benefit of the doubt.
But then you doubted the benefits that I could provide...so goodbye.
I can't take your annoying paranoia about what's hiding in the closet,
Even after I've given you the tour and shown you that there's nothing here but me.
I'm not going to waste my time with you second-guessing my sincerity and drive.
So whenever you get tired of the playground games and decide to grow up,
I'm sure there'll be someone else around to welcome you to the big league.

Tough to Love
Calloused fingers on guitar strings,
Calloused lips and tongue used to make you sing.
Both are proof that it takes rough times to perfect beautiful melodies.

The Denial Pile

The greatest dishonor that a writer can give someone
Is to be inspired enough by you to put ink to paper,
And then erase all traces of it.
You are no longer considered worthy of the memory
Or the immortality of script.
No longer worth caring about,
Welcome to the denial pile.

Squandered Wish

I shouldn't have asked for wisdom.

I thought it would help me, but all it really did was hurt me.

Sure, I was considered a wise guy and could outsmart the smartest,

But that also meant that I could justify anything to anybody including myself.

Loss Report

I'm sorry to bother you,
But I seemed to have lost my bag.
It's extremely important that I find it as soon as possible.

It's a burgundy, leather briefcase with handles at the top and a shoulder strap.
Scratches have pulled back some of the dye, leaving the base exposed.
The bag has been dragged and dropped so many times that the bottom looks black,
Like the belt straps attached to tighten the magnetic clasps that keep it snapped shut.
It makes it easier to close than to open, yet papers are constantly bursting at the seams.
The inside is heavily padded with black velvet
With red specks stuck on the middle divider.
Be careful not to reach too far inside because the side pockets have hook latches.

That's where I used to keep drafts of inventions,
Stored away the books that I was reading
With at least one of my favorites included:
Curtains, The Death of Superman, Knightfall,
And Then There Were None,
Or one of my favorite Choose-Your-Own-Adventure books.

Looking back, they almost seem like scripts for the future,
Volumes of the Pick-Your-Poison series of events that led to what I hold close.
I'm afraid that someone might have picked it up when it was left unattended,
Or even worse that I might have hid it from myself trying to be too clever for my own good.
That's why I'd constantly check to make sure nothing's changed since my last visit,
Always adding to it to ensure that I don't forget any important details.

I've been doing that for so long that now all it contains is tabloid confessions:
Half-written, scattered apologies for exasperating hope and breaking hearts,
Receipts for regrets,
Notes and numbers on bar napkins that I never bothered to use.
I record my feelings in love letters never sent.
The oldest being the one to the pre-med nurse
That let me walk her to the bottom of her hill after school.

I wonder what's become of that girl that I used to share the bus with.
Most of my writings detail what I would've said and done
If I wasn't too strong to hold myself back.
I often held back when she needed it the most
Because I didn't want to find my strength to be insufficient for the task
Or to save her so easily that she's convinced that I've been handling her with kid gloves.
I use the same gloves when holding my conspiracy theories and stories never told.
I can't leave fingerprints.
Because the night that I started my pursuit of higher education
Was the same night that I started creating smoke screens to hide the real me.

So I'm asking you to do me a favor.
I'm sure that you have many more important things to do,
But please keep an eye out for my bag.
If you find it,
Burn it.
Leave no traces of its existence except for a patch big enough for identification
But small enough to get easily lost.
Because I know that if you return it to me intact,
I'll never look at you the same,
Always paranoid of if you ever looked inside of it.
If I get it back, I'm afraid I'll keep adding to it
Until it stretches and tears,
Forming the fabric of the door mat for a room full of regrets.
The goal is to make sure that I don't find
Or ever create a replacement griefcase.

Late Night Ramblings

"Do you ever wonder if some of what we consider fiction is actually fact?"

Worst Case Scenario

A word to the wise:
Don't leave a thinker alone
Too long with his thoughts.

Perception
People don't realize
We're often figments of our
Imagination.

Insomniac

I can't go to sleep
I am afraid I'd meet me
And drive him insane.

A Prism of Personalities

I have a quiet and sweet side,
A fun and crazy side,
And the side where they intersect:
The quiet and crazy side.

Sacrificed

I wonder how many poems have been lost.
Plucked from my brain by the writing fairies,
Turned into unwilling sacrifices to the muses.

Sometimes they are gracious enough to return stolen lines,
Or leave me with better replacements.
Mounds of crumpled paper and boulders of crushed lead
Are waiting to be chiseled into stories.

Inheritance

What if you gained attributes or had your luck influenced
By all those who interacted with you in your infancy?
From rubs on your mother's belly to celebrating the first birthday,
Your aura absorbed love, wishes, and luck
As well as hate, ill will, and shortcomings.
How would your life turn out?
How would your parents let your life be influenced?

Origins

I don't know how it started, or if my origins are still being written.
All I know is that I'm a poet that needs someone else to help define me
Because a hero never thinks he's good enough and a villain doesn't see
what's so bad about the ends that justify the means.

I started off as nothing special, the nerdy one, constantly looked over and
forgotten.
One day I was bitten by a love bug, and before long, cooties set in.
I found myself gifted with empathy and understanding the human psyche.
I exiled myself to foreign cultures to study the science of my powers
And to learn how to harness the magic of the unknown but all too familiar.

I returned to use my gifts to the best of my abilities, trying save them all,
But I was unappreciated by too many who put themselves back in their same
situations.
Others looked down on me, thinking that I'm looking down on them,
Or that I'm just flaunting what I have for recognition, so they shunned me
worse than before.

Dark thoughts started to fill my lonely nights.
With no one that can relate or ease the pain,
My sacrifices seem more and more in vain.
So why don't I just worry about myself?
I seem to have a hero complex that's complicated by the fact that I'm a
realist who sometimes can relate to the bad guy.
I've grown to have a backdraft temper, which is unleashed when you open
your mouth after sucking all of the patience out of me.

In the quiet before the storm, I'm filled with curious contemplations.
I wonder how many bad guys started out good,
How the light stays bright surrounded by darkness,
And if I should keep trying to fight the good fight,
Or if I should throw in the towel and watch them sweat a little bit…

Half of Everything

There once was a man who found a lamp that contained a genie.
The genie told him, 'I'm not like the ones in the stories.
'You get three days to make as many wishes as you want, but your ex will get twice as much of everything that you wish for yourself.'
"Everything, you say? This could be fun," the man thought.

The man went right to work saying, "In that case, I wish that I had $5 billion."
He looked in his account and there it was.
For the next two days, he fulfilled all of his lifelong dreams.
Big houses, a lot full of cars, fame, traveling, and more.

On the third day, after lunch with his favorite celebrity crush,
He remembered that another man ruined his last relationship,
So he started thinking about his ex and spent the rest of his time dedicating wishes to her.

Among his most creative wishes, he wished that he found his soul mate,
Had a limp in one leg,
And that he needed to find a bathroom to take a #1 every hour on the hour through an eight hour stretch of nothing but desert.
On that same trip, he requested the genie to give him a flat tire in the rain with half the battery drained on his phone.

As the end of his wishing spree came to a close, the genie chimed in,
'I almost forgot to mention that after your three days are up, your ex immediately gets the same deal as you:
Three days, unlimited wishes, and you get twice as much.
Oh, and she'll know that you had my lamp before her.'
The man simply smiled and replied,
"In that case, I wish I couldn't use half of my motor skills for the next three days."

Never Land on the Second Star
To hell with Peter Pan.
Yea, I said it.
Damn his immaturity and selfishness.
I certainly will take it harder than you can imagine because we started off as
friends.

He helped a lonely kid survive being the new guy at school,
Made tougher by being the youngest in his class.
Pan was the tutor for Troublemaking 101.
Oh, the memories and mischief that we caused.

A rebel with a single cause.
"Let's give them something to talk about" was his motto.
He didn't understand why I wanted to stay grounded yet claimed to want to
soar.
It's probably because his head was constantly in the clouds, high off of pixie
sticks and rum.

One day, he brought a girl around who had a voice like a lullaby.
I tried to warn her about Lily and the Belle that he sometimes tinkered with,
But he convinced her to fly away with him.
He called her his darling and said that he felt closer to her than his own
shadow.
But I know how slippery that can be.
They would provide for him in return for all of his attention,
Until he found another, better adventure.

He didn't take it very well when I left.
He said that I felt like I had outgrown him.
I had just decided to grow up, while he still acts like a kid,
But it still hurt losing my right hand.
I hate that I had to leave him with the rest of the lost boys.

Fairly Tell It From the Dark Side

With so many lies being put out as truths,
Do you ever wonder if some of what we consider fiction is actually fact?
Believe me, it's amazing what a little cosmetics and misdirection can do.
Don't be alarmed but there's a good chance that you narrowly escaped a
monster's grasp today.

You might have walked right past a mad genius that you'll never hear about
because the look doesn't match the talent.
They keep to themselves, along with the invisible ones,
Those that you don't think twice about because you can see right through
them.
Be careful because you can easily forget that they're there until they make
their presence felt.

There's nothing like the wrath of the scorned.
But what about the ones you see coming but don't recognize the danger until
it's too late?
I've met a few that look like they could pass for royalty but have left many
stringing curses together when they found what was kept under wraps.
Some move fast while others stay at a zombie's pace,
But in the end they are all just looking for some brains.

The hard part of avoiding them is that you can't run because as soon as you
slow down or look over your shoulder, there they are.
Their population has grown so much that they're everywhere and have
blended in well.
There are some that obviously doctor themselves to spark interest,
Yet they're still weak imitations of life, made up of parts of others:
An outfit from the last award show, hairstyle from that one movie,
The swagger from that one guy who has that one song, and the opinions of
the town twit
…I mean twitter.

Others' true nature usually aren't revealed until you're in too deep,
Like the dark and lovely ones that prove to be all too good to be true.
Revealing an almost completely different person, they can no longer hide
once the veil has been lifted.
Lifted like the nose of those who can smell the scent of the hurt, the young,
the oblivious, and the tired.
I don't know if werewolves really exist, but werehumans sure do.

Dogs of both genders will leave you wondering where their humanity went when their fangs are bared.
Some nights are haunted by lonely thoughts of relationships and questions that just won't pass on,
Just like those who go ghost when you need them the most,
Only to reappear at the most inconvenient times.

I just wanted to take the time to warn you about those and the most dangerous ones,
The sirens that are looking to smash you against the rocky bottom, so that they can collect the shattered pieces.
Their sweet voices will talk you right into danger, and you'll put yourself at risk,
Unable to resist, seeing the signs but saying, "It'll be all right, I can handle this."

I'm not saying all of this to scare you.
I just wanted to shake things up and see what you'll do with the information.
And for those who will get mad that I've exposed them, I have my share of bodies in the closet.
I can't even look my reflection in the eye, but I've learned to live with it.
Just like some will live to learn that my bark is smoother than my bite,
And that I won't cross boundaries unless invited to first.
Call me up to bat and you can count on me to be a gentleman until the sweet end.
So if you hope to survive a monster encounter,
Keep your wits about you, and try not to look like such an easy target.

A Chat With A Shinigami

My man!

It's been a minute.

I haven't seen you since that time you got introduced to Romulus and almost forgot how to breathe.

Hahaha, you can never really trust college frat boys,

There's no telling what's in their stuff.

Ah, good times...well, that's pretty rude.

What do you mean, what am I doing here?

Isn't it obvious,

I'm just trying to catch up with you, and it wasn't too hard with you leaving a trail with all that leaking.

Anyways, you're looking good...well not really.

The whole pez neck isn't a good look...

Wait, what did you think I was talking about when I said that you were leaking?

Are you that drunk, that you thought you could knock the knife away, open a rigged door, and jump out of a moving car all in one quick move?

Hahaha of course you are, you must have been to think that it'd be ok to ride alone in a taxi front seat...

Yea, so what if you had three other people in there with you when you started this trip.

You didn't think to jump in the back after the last one got dropped off?

Made too much sense?... hehe...

Hey, don't get mad at me, I'm just stating the obvious.

Anyways, it is what it is and what's done is done.

So the real question is, what are you going to do now?

You can't call anyone because your phone's been dead most of the night.

You can't flag anyone down because who's up at 4 in the morning?

You're steady leaking and you're still 12, 11 blocks from where you're staying.

I'm not that great with math but those aren't the best odds homie...

You're just going to walk it off?

Hahaha that's a good one.

You see, that's what I like about you, you always got jokes.

I'm curious to see what you'll do now.

You can't run or else your heart will pump blood faster,

But you can't take too long because you've had quite a bit to drink,

So your blood's already running thin.

Don't trip, we can play my favorite game to take your mind off of it.
It's called 'What's the last color you see?'
It ends differently for everybody,
So let me know if you see a bright light or if everything fades to black.
Afterwards, we can leave for the party that I've been planning in your honor,
I even got a limo.
You'll want to wear your best suit.
Trust me, it'll be the party of a lifetime.
People will fly in last minute just to be a part of it.
Women are going to be weak in the knees, crying, throwing themselves all over you.
Someone will probably read one of your poems, or maybe even write one in your honor to go with the plaque and flowers that you'll receive.
And don't think it's over after that, there's still the after party.
It'll be in either the Red Room or the White Room.
I know that both wanted you to RSVP,
So I guess you probably know which one better suits you.

…Really?
After all that, you're gonna ditch me just because you made it home?
That's messed up… well at least I have more time to plan your party.
We'll have it eventually, so I'll catch you later.
Remember, third time's the charm.

New Gods

Our Father, which art in the cloud,
DaBigBoss be thy handle.
Give us this day our daily memes.

You prepare a thread before me in the presence of my haters.
You anoint my page with the block and privacy features.
My direct messages runneth over.
Surely LOLs and Emojis shall follow me
All the days of my timeline.

I thank you that I'm not like the ratchets,
And those that do it for the vine,
I ain't gonna do it.
I ain't gonna do it for the followers,
Though I am linked in with many connections.

As I examine my selfie,
Help me watch my words, 140 characters at a time.
Forgive my reckless posts and tags,
As I forgive the cyber stalking, spam game invites, and messages taken out
of context.
And do not lead us into temptation,
But deliver us from the evil ones,
The internet thugs throwing up hashtags and idle threats,
The conspiracy theorists that rant from behind the fence of internet anomaly,
As well as the models that hide behind filters and Photoshop.
Because the thirst is real.
But that's none of my business.

Though I walk through the valley of the shadow of posts,
I will fear no incriminating screenshots, for thou art with me.
Your likes and your shares, they comfort me.

Thy will be done on Wi-Fi, as it is on hardline.
In the name of the Facebook, the Instagram, and ever present Twitter,
#Amen.

The Creation Bomb

On the morning of the first day,
There was a great rumble and a dark cloud seeped from beneath the surface
of Eden across the globe.
That was considered the start of the last days and the beginning of the eternal
night.

On the second day, there was no more sunlight.
The sky became dark and the seas became turbulent.
By the third day, floods drowned the land and plants.
Those that survived quickly withered with the kiss of the contamination.

The fourth day brought the last glimmer of light and hope.
The haze covering the sky thickened, and the stars and planets blinked out
one by one.
On the fifth day, the contamination spread to the sea and all of the fish swam
to the surface,
Becoming easy prey for the birds,
Which silenced the chirps.

By the sixth day, the last of mankind scrambled to save the animals that they
could from the infections.
It spread almost faster than the fear and panic.
No one knows what killed the last one standing.
Was the killer imaginary, microscopic, or one that looked all too familiar?
The only answer was silence on the seventh day.
All of the chaos led to peace and a rest that hovered over the stillness.

With the destruction of everything within a seven day timeframe,
A devil tried to become like God.
He looked on his work and saw that it was good.

C is for Complicated

C is for confirmations and contradictions.
O is for opportunities and oppositions.
M is for magic and misdirection.
P is for pleasure and pain.
L is for laughter and languish.
I is for inspiration and isolation.
C is for clarification and convolution.
A is for authentic and artificial.
T is for triumph and tragedy.
E is for everlasting and ending.
D is for desire and distraction.

The Lost Ones

"Years of memories streamed down his face…"

21 Gun Salute

Sleep deprived but still on a high from the night before,
I got the call.
Waking up with a smile, I expected to hear her voice,
But the tone was much deeper.
"Doc...he's gone...Canon's gone."

I don't remember what he said next
Because I had already started scrambling for the exit to this nightmare,
Only to find both of my parents coming into the room with looks that
confirmed my fear.
My brother was dead.

Growing up together in the church,
All he ever wanted was to make a difference and to not be a statistic,
Which is why he left for school as soon as he turned 18.
So why, a week before he finished his freshman year,
Did he have to be the third wheel on Bonnie and Clyde's date night?
Did they have to double back after he was already in the rearview?
Why would they think that there'd be something worthwhile in his turned out
pockets?
Why did they leave him bleeding in the dark on the side of the road?

They assassinated the one that we called Diplomat in our crew.
My heart dropped to half-mast.
I couldn't find the strength to check on anyone,
Not even my best friend.
I just hoped that her plane was already in the air,
And that she could be on Cloud 9 for at least a little while longer.

I lost my voice trying to translate screams and moans
Into the language of angels and spirits,
Trying to call my friend back to us.

That day, we took the Bay Area hostage.
Heads tucked into knees,
We became Canon balls,
Ready to explode and shower everything in shattered grief.
Lips quivering almost as much as itchy trigger fingers.
Tears fell like the ash of fuses
That were triggered by cell phones.
We were spread out in so many places,

From bathrooms to class rooms,
Airports, schools, businesses, and government buildings.

Though time stood still, news traveled fast.
Those that he stood by
Stood in a packed church to say bye.
Some even flew across coasts to pay respects.
By the end of his service,
There wasn't a dry eye or comprehendible word.

Most people there to pay their respect were held together by tissue and
crumbling supports,
The same ones that would be considered pillars of society on any other day.
Teachers, officers, reporters, and ministers were all in tears.
All shared the feeling that there's nothing worse than trying to be strong
For someone else when falling apart yourself.

But you have to be strong when most of the pallbearers are younger than 21.
Uneven breathing from choking back sobs,
Hands slippery from wiping away tears,
Yet there wasn't a loose grip among us.
We had promised to not let him down,
That we would carry our brother to that hearse
No matter how much it hurts.

We didn't let him down.
We still hold that promise and the one to not become statistics.
Instead, we've become college graduates,
Admission counselors, managers, preachers, bankers, and community
leaders.
We still salute our brother, Canon Jones II,
By living life to the fullest,
And trying to make this world a better place.

Fighting Time

No longer wishing to keep composure or caring what others thought,
There he sat.
Years of memories streamed down his face,
Yet he didn't say a word.
The only sound that came from his table was the occasional sob,
That sounded more like he was mid-laugh and trying to catch his breath,
With a hand attempting to massage a smile onto his face.

I wanted to say something,
But I was at a loss for words as much as he was,
Then our eyes met.
All I could do was nod,
A solemn gesture of support.
He smiled a quiet thank you and tried to blink away the fog.

As I left, he beckoned me over.
He showed me a timeless photo in his pocket watch as he watched time pass.
"It's been a week since I said goodbye to my wife.
I've lived longer with her than I've lived by myself.
It's been a lot quieter than I thought it'd be.
If you haven't met her yet,
I hope that you'll one day find someone as special as my sweet Mary."
I thanked him and started looking for her.

Guilty Love

I once met a man that only had one hand.
He kept fumbling between his drink and his phone,
Then our eyes met.
I tried offering a sympathetic smile,
But he laughed it off.

"I'm not used to using my left,
But I lost the right to my right.
If you're wondering why I don't have a prosthetic,
It's because I want the strange looks."

"I used to pride myself on my calm demeanor,
But that night we had a bad fight…
Such a bad, stupid fight…
I don't even remember how it started.
We both said things that we probably didn't mean.
Next thing I knew she was banging on my chest.
I tried to hold onto her,
But she pulled away and hit me in my eye.
That's when I lost it.
Half blind trying to find her,
Half of me was trying to get my bearings
And the other half saw red.
Before I knew it, all arguments were silenced and she was on the ground.
Still staggering, I went tumbling after her trying to make amends.
Already halfway up when I was on my way down,
She stormed out in tears…
I never got the chance to apologize.
There was an accident about a mile out,
And she died on the scene."

"The next morning, I found comfort in Matthew 5:30,
'And if your right hand causes you to sin, cut it off and throw it away.
For it is better that you lose one of your body parts
Than that your whole body go to hell.'"

A Note to Precious

I won't start by saying that I'm missing your presence.
Though you're gone, you'll always be present
In the hearts and minds of those you've touched,
Even those who dared to say you were ever doing too much.

They say that the good ones always die young,
But nobody really knows when their time will come.
So it's necessary to always live life to its fullest potential,
And it's a shame that this world only had you as a rental.

Only a short time, before your time here was through,
No late fee would have been too great to have a little more time with you.
Just one more chance for conversations late into the night,
Silly jokes, and to see that smile that shines so bright.
But now the room seems a little bit dimmer
Without that signature grin that made everyone feel like a winner.

I know that you wouldn't want anybody to feel down that you aren't here
Because you always did things to make others' frowns disappear
And leave nothing but smiles and laughter in your wake.
That's why I always thought you were so great.
A trait that seems so hard to find,
You always cared so much about others but didn't at the same time.
You hated seeing other feeling bad,
But loved seeing the haters get mad
At the way you moved and styled yourself in colors so bold
Showing that you knew you were royalty whether in purple or gold.

So I dedicate this to a sister and a friend, who will always be missed,
A life that will forever be felt and remembered just like a hug and a kiss.

Oz

A wiz of a mastermind,
He sent her over the rainbow
With just his words.

He took her heart,
Then he stole her confidence,
So he could get some brains.

Only someone with the head the size of a room
Would have the gall to send a country girl into the lion's den,
Simply on a whim
Because it seemed like a good idea at the time.

The Broken Ones

I love the broken ones,
Equipped with a complimentary excuse to end our time together at a
moment's notice.
I find the ones not so broken that it's obvious,
But the ones held together by glue, not masking tape.
It better masks the taped off areas of memories and scars
That are prone to crumble under applied pressure.
That makes it easy to hide my broken pieces among her remains,
To escape the isolation of my self-deconstruction,
Picked apart piece by piece trying to find solace.
We find our own.

Second Best

She never thought that she'd be a warning track.
As the obtuse side of a love triangle,
She found herself at the mercy of someone else's schedule.
He said that he couldn't really call or meet due to the nature of his work,
When he really just worked her nature knowing that she trusted him.

She wasn't supposed to fall for him.
A random meeting led to intense feelings.
Slowly but surely he learned her
And she learned pain.

He lived in both sides of an alternate reality,
One with her,
And the other in a committed marriage with kids.
He had the best of both worlds until his lady called his lady.
She learned that the secret that he kept from her was that she was the secret.

The random thoughts that used to lead to smiles,
Now end in tears in the middle of the day.
The pain of the shame didn't stop her from accepting his phone calls.
He tried to explain the context of their relationship,
But it just clouded her state of mind.
She felt like she should've known by his lack of commitment
That she would come out a casualty in their casual relationship.

But she was what he's been missing,
Why else would he have looked somewhere else for affection?
But since the revelations,
Their relationship has hit complications.
The calls become less frequent.
She wonders if he found a replacement for his replacement,
Or if he just decided that it wasn't worth the secrets, the sneaking, the lies, and the risks.
She wanted to confront him
But didn't dare to find out that she wasn't really worth it.
With her trust seared to the nerve,
Now she'd rather jump to conclusion then fall for another trap too hard to bear.

Hurting

She presses her head slowly against the pillowcase,
Hoping that the pressure will stop the swelling in her face.
Another argument ended with her on the floor,
Even after he said again and again that it wouldn't happen anymore.

She was burned again by the flare of his temper.
He apologized as his boiling point began to simmer.
He said that he doesn't know why he lashes out and she doesn't know why she accepts his "mistakes."
She just steadied herself, told him that it's fine, and put on a smile that they both know is fake.

What she really wanted to do was just let it all out, cry and show him how hurt she feels.
She doesn't though because she doesn't know how he'll respond or if his response will even be real.
She already knew that he'd say that he's sorry, things will get better, and that he loves her.
How can that be when her heart skips a beat, flinching, whenever he moves too quickly but only trying to touch her?

As she breathes slowly, her head stops pounding at last
From the pain at least but not from the questions that should be asked.
If that's how he treats her, how can it really be love?
Especially when he's mad, look at the things that he does
When it comes to other things that he holds dear.
When's the last time that he's hit his car's windshield making its vision blurry and unclear?
Or what about the times he threw the TV on the ground
Just because he was losing a fight or didn't like how it sound?
When did he ever leave his dog bruised and bloody because it didn't react quick enough to his commands?
And if ever questioned about any of it, he would just say, 'I don't know what happened, I just know I that couldn't let that stand.'

She tries to answer those questions and can't remember an instant of him ever doing any of those things.
So she starts crying, not knowing if it's because of that truth or because of the pain as her ears continue to ring.
Ringing like the wedding bells that she had once imagined hearing as they walked down the aisle.

49

Now she just feels trapped, everyday waking up in a constant state of denial.

She hopes that he'll get better because she doesn't want to leave him,
And if she stays optimistic, at least she'll have half a mind to believe him.
She loves him, and doesn't love include all of the deficiencies?
But she thinks twice, after hearing about Rihanna being compared to Whitney.

On top of all of that, just like all divorces, he'd still get half.
Half of the things that they bought together, half of the memories of times she's laughed,
Half of the reason for why half of her future relationships won't work,
While the other half is from her fears of how she could get hurt,
And the reason for half of the scars that she's gained in her lifetime,
The physical and emotional ones that keep her crying at night.
At least half of the rest of tonight
Could be spent listing the halves he would take for the rest of her life.

Through the silent sobs and tears, she tries thinking of ways to fix this,
But every time she has an idea, she thinks of ways he would leave it twisted.
If she ever thought of taking some time away from him,
It would be like taking a dog to a meat house and unchaining him.
She doesn't trust him as far as he can throw her,
Especially if he's around his boys and a little past sober.
She's thought about and even suggested that they go to therapy,
But he keeps saying, 'Ah, I don't want anyone in my head but you baby.'
Plus, she knows if they go, he'll act right only for a while or until her satisfactions are fed,
And she doesn't like surprises and would rather be able to see it coming instead
Of her letting her guard down and not even being able to brace herself
From the blow or him saying, 'Sorry, but I told you that it wouldn't work. I just can't help myself.'

He'll crack that signature smile that's just a little bit sinister,
Knowing that everything's ok even after he's left her lip splintered.
Because she'll forgive him, at least that's what she said
After he beat her physically, while she's doing the same in her own head.
She feels ashamed and hates herself for not having the strength to stand up to him or to leave.
Her and many other people don't understand that it also takes strength to admit that you're weak.

50

Jesus didn't come for the healthy and strong, but for the tired and hurt.
She needs someone to save her from him and herself, before she believes that she's only getting what she deserves,
Someone who can take her away, tend to her wounds, and will stay by her side like a Good Samaritan.
Otherwise, she might have so many scabs that she becomes a shell of her former self in the end,
Nothing but a living scar, tough on the outside but fragile and broken within.

The Wrong One
I woke up with her straddling my hips.
She told me, 'Baby, you f'd with the wrong girl.'
Right before cold steel froze my pose.

Ours eye met
And for a moment,
We finally moved as one.
We looked down to where her hands cradled my butterflies,
With sound bouncing off the hollows of cocoon coffins that weren't
supposed to be opened.
I don't know who laughed and who gasped for air.
I couldn't believe I hadn't woken up yet,
And she couldn't believe that she went through with it.

It wasn't so long ago
That at her best she was love,
But other times she was a mirror of what she'd see.
She left when I was right during arguments.
She became upset and paranoid when I took her at her word,
No interrogation was conducted but I was still booked as a bad cop.
Labeled unfeeling as a terminator,
She called me silent and deadly to her heart.
When I was quiet, she tried to fill in my blanks with 'you should be…why
don't you…'
After a while, I'd mute her voice by raising the volume of mine.
We said that we were determined to find how things were supposed to be.
Why were we burning out instead of bright?
She'd insist on second helpings and dessert
When I was borderline sick of what she cooked up,
Especially when she'd find excuses or pulled away when I showed interest.

Which brings us to now.
Intestines leaking their content like she wanted to prove that I was full of
shit.
I already knew that she had let friends or her own thoughts convince her that
I was cheating,
When I was really just scheming.
I didn't want her looking in my phone because she would've seen the
numbers that I called for reservations.
I wonder if I wasn't as slick as I thought and was seen with a "mystery"
woman.

I used my cousin to get a lady's perspective on the ring sitting in my dresser drawer.

This wasn't how my breath was supposed to be taken away.
Like always, she realized her power over me too late for comfort
But too soon for forgiveness as apologies gush.
And like always, I try to be strong for her.
I try to say, "I love you."
But it gurgles out, "Fuv you."
I hardly even feel it, could hardly see, and barely hear muffled screams.
The world's on mute.

Looking up, I could see the bright of her halo,
Hovering over my body warmed by the devil's robe,
Draped in light and a blanket of red.
Is that sirens or the wail of a siren?

King's Game

She let him make the first move,
And then that block queen gave birth to a chess piece,
A pawn spawned to aid in the game of keeping her king.

He started to become more distant,
So she added two more pawns to her ranks to stack her odds.
But she soon realized that her king was just castling,
Jumping space to space, ready to sacrifice whatever and whoever for his own purposes.
A woman scorned can easily make for a bitter queen, poisoning the fairy tale ending for the children.

As time went by, they grew under her influence.
The oldest grew to become a bishop but saw the world crookedly,
A scar across his face from when he first crossed his father.

His brother had a slightly better view of life because he built armor around his heart.
He was seen as an L7 because he sidesteps trouble and the unnecessary,
Though sometimes that included friends and family.

The youngest, who was the most protected and looked after,
Seemed like a straight shooter.
Yet he played the role of a rook turning others into pros,
Beat to the punch and captured for his cause.

And so went the tale of a queen, her bishop, knight, and rook,
All with the same aim in mind:
"All hell to the king."
The moral of the story is to always check out your potential mate
Before getting too deep into the game.

His Story Revisited

Close your eyes.
Now imagine that this is how you see the summer sun,
With a nose so congested that breathing through it sounds like you're being strangled.
That's how Little Marcus walked around too many days of his young life.

Allergic to plants is what his mom would say to explain away the looks when they went out,
With the severity of his reaction endorsed by his grass-stained sports pants.
He played outfield and catcher, but it was outside the field of normal gameplay that he caught his condition.
You could try asking his father about it, but all that would be found is the dusty spot reserved for his love.

Work kept him away for stretches at a time,
Hardly home, and when he was there it was hardly a home.
So the son became the defender of the house.
Chin up, chest out, slow breaths to keep composure…
But he blinks, heart skipping a beat,
Right before God's name is used, but not for bless yous.
There's silence before, "He was asking for it."
And he was.

He was told to stay out of grown folks business because this is between him and her,
But he's the result of the union between him and her,
So he stands between him and her trying to intercede.
Not caring about his own well-being, he knew that he's allergic to his father's touch,
Which can result in body aches, blood-clotted nose, or eyes swollen shut,
Leaving him sometimes blind as a bat, yet able to pick out sobs through two doors, a hallway, and a pillow trying to plug the leak in her watery eyes.
The same eyes that met his, which asked why locks and alarms never changed or why they didn't just leave.
It's because he has the key to her heart, she told him, "Baby, sometimes those that make you the happiest, hurt you the worst."

He knew then that love would be the death of one of them,
Especially once he overheard that it was supposed to have gotten better after he was born.
Thinking that the son was to bear the iniquity of the father,

He offered his skin for his father's sin, to atone for his tone.
But he began to resent the fact that he never did repent,
Even after trying in vain to use his heart to jumpstart the one inside his old man.
Marcus became aged beyond his years, gray hairs crowned his head.
Most people would notice these instead of the thinly veiled lies of what lied beneath the veil of why he never invited friends over.

This only made the seed of hate grow faster that the Old Man had planted within the seed given to his mate.
Letting it grow uneasy under the family tree, until it fully festered, like the Addams family *snap snap*
But no one gives a damn about family values when those snaps were his wrist and arm against the stairs.
It might be unsettling, but his family has never been the settling down type.
Yet, even at their most riled up, it's spooky how calm he can be.

A kid with a kooky sense of humor, like the time he woke up his father to share the enlightenment of why he was called Marcus.
"Because you want to continue to mark us with your legacy."
The Old Man lost that battle, but he refused to lose the war,
Which left Marcus waking up in the hospital a week later with all the familiar symptoms,
And the Old Man gone again for another stretch but this time indefinitely.

They say all's well that ends well...
Well, I've also heard that apples don't fall far from the tree.
So to keep from rotting out, he remembers his roots.
Not that anyone would ever let him forget.
Everywhere he goes, he's recognized as his father's child.
The spitting image, but every chance he got he would spit on his image.
Marcus decided to be the mirror reflection, flipped to be the exact opposite,
To change his legacy, to become a generational composite.
He inherited the temper of father, which constantly fights with the patience that he learned from his mother.
Years later their conflict still wages on,
Held at bay by his drink of choice,
The same one that his grandfather used to use to fuel his voice.

He uses it in the same way, knowing that everyone deserves to have at least one person speak up in their defense.

He didn't have that because when he tried to be there for her, his voice went unheard,
So he decided to be the voice of the unheard if only to ensure that someone hears and cares.

That's why he uses soft words to cushion his sharp edges.
He became a love poet, but love can make you do some crazy things.
Just a quiet guy, with a hidden darker side, who takes time with what he says
Because he still gets a little choked up sometimes.
I guess the only thing really left to say is to thank his old man for making him who he is today.

He Could've Been A Contender
He could have been the next Willie Brown,
A politician, a star athlete, a musician,
Or even the first one that comes to mind when you mention that name.
But when his name is mentioned among some, the joy leaves the room.
Those happy thoughts were buried along with his potential.

He'll forever be addressed in the media by his victim's name to increase his shame,
Twenty-three years old when he lost the rest of his life for stripping a 2-year-old of his.
What happened to people acting their age or like they have some sense?
We went from kids just being kids to being Toys "R" Us Kids,
Never wanting to grow up, everything is all fun and games,
Taking nothing serious, until they find out that there are no refunds, exchanges, or rain checks for consequences.

Instead of bonding over ABCs or 123s, he taught him that ABCs are as easy as 123s.
For those who don't know that's Alternating Body and Chin shots are as easy as 1-2-3 combos.
So he strapped him up with a pair of boxing gloves for a round of Rock 'Em Sock 'Em.
Fifteen minutes in, Willie's head rocked back against the wall, then the floor, and he's down for the count.

He was left brain-dead, but I guess Willie wanted it to be like father like son,
With the apple not falling too far from the tree, laying within eye view.
He waited at least 30 minutes for an idea to breakthrough for a better way for this story to conclude.
It was the babysitter, in the bedroom, with an unknown object was how his father explained the situation.
When asked if that was his final answer, he admitted to just wanting to teach his son how to box.
He wasn't going to teach him the underappreciated side of being a man,
Like hitting the water and not the seat, tying a tie, shaving,
How to be a man of your word, or how to treat a lady.
He wanted him to know how to fight before he could even speak.
It's no wonder that so many grow up wanting to settle arguments with fists, instead of using their words to talk things out.

What happened to make so many grow up with more hits than hugs?
More *puff* hits than hugs, more *sniff* hits than hugs,
More *dose* hits than hugs, more *arm tap* hits than hugs,
More quick fixes and sad shrugs to the question of what happened to us.

What happened to make it ok for a mother to go on the news to say,
'I don't think my son was capable of that. He might be capable of beating the boy's mother,
But they always go at it, but then she goes right back to him.'
What happened to bettering ourselves and trying to do more than just survive?
What happened?

Real Talk
This is not a threat
Or a promise.
It's a fact.
If I ever see you again,
I won't just kill you,
I will mangle you.

I will make you scream in pitches that you didn't even know that you had.
I will arrange body parts like a Picasso and Dali joint painting.
I will negate your hold on reality.
Up will be down, light will be dark, and death will be welcomed.
I will grind the hope from your very essence.
I will liquefy all that is solid and scab over all that is soft.
I will erase all of your thoughts and memories of everything except pain, my face, and why we met.
Then and only then will I put you down.

The Doctor Is In

Wakey wakey, it's time to get started.
We're here because you left someone brokenhearted.
You're the reason behind all of her unnecessary pain and duress.
O where are my manners? My name is Dr. Loveless
Welcome to the Looking Glass, where I do my best work.
It's a nightmare for some, but a sanctuary for all those who've been hurt.

Sorry for having to incapacitate you before we could be alone,
But like you probably told someone else, I got a girl at home.
I brought you to this place, my room full of mirrors,
So we can both reflect and see things a bit clearer.
You see, some say that the eyes are a gateway to the soul,
So I'm going to help you look at yours and the part of hers that you stole.

You can go ahead and give me the whole "don't hate the player, hate the game,"
But consider me the league's enforcer to make sure that you're not let back into the game.
I love the game, but like all things the players can bring it shame
Because the game can be corrupted and it's only as good as how it's played.
How do you call yourself a player but cheat to take the prize without permission?
You took her love, her trust, her hope, and so much more and left it all twisted.
It's been written that two shall be joined and become one,
But you ripped that apart and took parts of her when you were done.

Though she deserves so much more, she feels much less than worthy
Because of what you took when you tricked her with your sorcery.
You were her shining knight bringing a love that to her was magic,
But she found that magic can sometimes be an illusion and that your suit still had its rental tags.
Which finally brings us to you and me.
We've talked about yours, so now listen to my history.
Cupid doesn't like what he sees with all that's been done
In his name, and he truly is his father's son.
The Son of Ares, war personified.
His father's motto is let no enemy survive,
Or at least make them an example to leave others petrified,
Which led Cupid to you and you to I.

61

And now that we have had our introductions, it's time to begin.
I'll go ahead and tell you what's in store from beginning to end.
Since you're so much of a "pimp," I'm going to give you that limp for real,
An arrow through each foot because besides the heart, it's the body part that takes the longest to heal.
Then you'll lose your eyelids, but I'll provide you with some Visine.
I don't want you to miss a blink or to try convincing yourself it's all a dream.
I'm going to throw salt in your game by throwing some in your eye,
So you can feel how she felt whenever you made her cried.

You say you're such a man, but you put your hands on her.
So I guess I'll have to be the real man and stand up for her.
For all the times that you'd shake her until she was bruised and sore,
What I'm going to do next is probably going to shake you to your core.
I'm going to take your dominant hand,
The one that you used to show her who's the boss and under your command.
But that's just the start because I also want your other hand,
So I can see which really does hurt more, when it's an open or clenched hand.

By that time, you'll probably pass out from the shock.
But I'll have you waking up feeling like you just fell off a dock.
All wet, washed up and gasping for air,
Even when I know you're awake, I'll continue to give you more water so that you can share
How she felt whenever you threatened to take her breath away
Or told her, 'you're smothering me, so take your drama and fall away.'

Plus, you'll need all this water to keep you hydrated.
You've lost enough fluids to keep you weak and sedated,
And we're only halfway done.
What I described was only the warm-up before I really have some fun.
I don't want to go into details, but I'll give you some highlights
Of what we'll both remember most about the rest of the night.

You'll lend me an ear so that I'll always have someone to talk to who won't judge me,
And so in the future you'll always have to pay close attention and listen more carefully.
I'm going to do something unmentionable to your unmentionables that I don't want to describe,

But let's just say that by the end you'll be screaming in a pitch, that for a
man would be too high.
And finally, they'll have to surgically remove your foot from ankle deep in
your ass
Because I'm going to implant it in there for good measures and a good laugh.

By that time I'll probably have worked up an appetite,
And I plan on being a good host so I'll be polite.
I'll give you a mix of shrooms and acid while I grab a bite and empty my
bladder,
And leave you here with your dreams and hers that you shattered.

At some point, you'll probably ask why I've done all of this,
And I'll ask why you haven't been paying attention, but the other big reason
is this...
I have a mom, a sister, a wife, and one day maybe a baby girl,
And I refuse to let her deal with such a crazy world.
Worthless guys won't even think once about approaching her sideways
They'll say, "That's Mr. Solomon's baby girl, so stay way way away."
I plan to be known by rentalmen and gentlemen alike,
So the gentlemen will say, "He's a little crazy but he's alright."

64

Whiskey Tears

"…Nightcaps became my handicap."

Straight to Voicemail

Sometimes, I let it go straight to voicemail
Because I'm scared of the phone call
That I know is coming any day now.
The death of life as I know it.
I don't answer, so I can hear the news on my terms.

The Killing Joke

One bad day.
One bad night.
One bad week.
One bad month.
One of those is all that is needed to turn any ordinary person insane.

A creation of a series of unfortunate events,
Forced to run a maddening gauntlet:
Burnt breakfast, bills piling up, a flat tire,
A stain on that new shirt, can't quite keep up with deadlines,
Job loss, a cheating significant other, and you cracked your phone screen,
Which doesn't seem to stop all of the bad news coming in.

And so falls the final straw.
Some use all of this as motivation or as a time to reflect on the bright spots,
But I'm concerned with the ones who fall into the shadows.
Finally cracked and ready to be put on display,
Part of the freak show.
Come one, come all,
Come see the Fallen,
Doomed to paranoia and self-harming tendencies.

They willing give into their vices
Because it helps keep a grip on reality as they wished it would be.
It lets them be whoever they want, say whatever comes to mind,
And do what they want without hesitation.
Constantly pushed and pushing past their limits,
See how closely people watch their actions from a distance.

Everyone journeys into the smokers' lounge to ask why he lights his pipe.
It's to help keep the corners of his lips high.
He wants to seems untouchable,
Always cool and calm, unfazed by the world.
He's constantly dusting himself off, but no one really knows why.
He exhales ashes from being burnt out.
No one knows if the embers start from the outside in or from the inside out.
Such a crispy image, but oh so fragile.

His crate is right next to the drunk tank.
A bottle is kept on deck to help lubricate his voice and numb the
cottonmouth,

So he can say what is really on his heart.
With a dose of liquid courage but no solid ground to maintain balance,
He stays hung over the edge.

And on the edge of this lineup is the world's most eligible nun.
Holy she claims to be, but when asked about answered prayers, she has none.
Prays for a good man though you'll find her reasoning holey of why she
seems to find none.
She says that they are all the same,
But what else would you expect my dear if you meet them all at the clubs?
By default, don't you think that most of its regular clientele would share
similar qualities?
It's the same with the ones that she's met at bars and lounges.
They sit at the bar of standard, never trying to rise above their positions,
Happy to lounge around while she puts in time and emotions.
She just wants someone who will spend some time to understand her.
They say that she deserves better, but never said that they were the ones
willing to give it to her.

I give you a chance to see their sad predicaments,
As spectators make hindsight predictions.
Hear them say, "It all makes sense now…I had a feeling there was something
off with…"
But they had no idea.
Judgments are passed without reviewing their individual cases.
Community reporters mediating the flow of information
Makes it hard to keep your head up,
With new facts pouring in all the time
Changing the tide of opinions.

But their opinion never changes,
"You weren't saying anything to me in good times,
So why say something about me when it's all bad?
You may know my situation but not me,
So why would I want to hear what you have to say?"

Why why why why why?
Why indeed is what I ask.
Why is it so easy to tear people down?

I've learned that patience is a virtue,
And with it you can virtually convince people of anything.

Subtle nudges and repetition wears down even the hardest surface.
Put a hood over eyes to divert attention from the mastermind,
Implicate random tragedies, inconsiderate words, and heartless people
To persuade some that the world is nothing more than an awful joke,
And not worth fighting for.
They'll fail to realize that some things are just meant to happen
To ensure that they'll grow or help the people that they are supposed to.

The greatest joke that the devil pulled wasn't convincing people that he
didn't exist,
It was convincing you to believe that you are all alone.
It makes it easier to pick people off one by one.

Don't

Don't dare question me.
You don't know what I've been through,
So you can't judge me.

Through The Looking Glass

Hey there Darkness,
How are you?
I'm fine…
You didn't let me finish.
I'm finally fine accepting that I'm anything but fine.
I'll be tonight's entertainment, walking the fine line of day and night, dream and reality.
Every hope out of the ordinary jolts me back awake, gasping for air,
So I hold my breath to avoid drowning in this sea of madness,
But I've realized that you have to be a little crazy to make it around here.

There ain't always sunshine on this side of the moon,
I sit alone among the stars, trying to see what they are shooting for and to help them recognize their own shine.
But I can't always be that comforting smile and encouraging word.
Sometimes the craters on the dark side fill up and can no longer be iced over.
Sometimes I can't be me, and I just have to be myself.

I'll show you the best of all sides but for the worse purposes.
So I suggest that you tread lightly in my vicinity because I'm steppin sharply, leaving bloody footprints in my wake.
A Jack of Hearts with an axe to grind, where if turned upside down
You'd see that I'm nothing more than a bleeding spade,
A frown hidden by a handstand.
All tricks aside, even if you look in my eyes you still might see a disguise
Because you really don't understand me when I try to be clear.

I'm as deep as the shallow end of the sea.
I'll let you see straight to the bottom, but you still won't know me because you don't know what's underneath the sand and what's been washed away.
Who knows, you might find it through the looking glass that fell overboard,
Lost along with many tales from my journey left in the backwash of bottles.

Swallowed by the deep end, I kick back and just go with the flow
Because my GPS has turned into grainy static.
The station stays the same but always changes if you read between the lines.
Connect the dots to find that they are just dots connected by lines,
But half of the ones making the connections will say otherwise.
And therein lies the joke of illumination.
Hello Sunshine,
Please to make your acquaintance.

Silhouettes

They're always here,
Following me everywhere that I go.
Sometimes matching my stride,
Other times leading the way.
I try to be strong and look down on them,
And they'll leave for a while.
But they always come back,
Mocking my every move,
Knowing that there's nothing that I can really do
When they surround me or bring some friends that are twice my size as help.
I hate standing in the shadow of guilt.

Cain & Abel

Because I'm my own master, I'm a slave of self.
I constantly beat my body into submission,
But sometimes my mind is on the losing side.

Fallen prey to the dark side,
I am brother to the night like the son of Eve.
The morning son, crying over my sins
Because what I do hurts me,
And for what I want to do I find myself ableless.
I was able to do good until I was caned,
Abused by this world,
No longer willing to offer my flesh,
Only the fruits grown from the dirt thrown on me.

I started using Cain as my crutch to lean on,
Realizing too late that it handicapped me,
Killing my ability to function at my full capacity.

I have Abel's blood in my veins and now on my hands.
I'm marked for rejection because I'm not quite able
To keep my promises and fulfill my duty.
I once could and was accepted because of it,
But now I'm in a constant spiral of red and white…
Right and wrong…

I'm Abel…I'm Cain…I'm a bain to my own existence,
Neglecting what I say I'll do and doing what I say I'll neglect.
Sometimes Cain… sometimes Abel… sometimes a cable
Must be sent out for help and strength
Because though I can be Cain, I strive to be Abel.
I am my other's keeper.

The 4th Cometh

And in your weak times
I will take you by the hand,
And slap you with it.

Get it together.
We know you're stronger than this.
Make them know it too.

Heckle the Jekyll

From time to time, I go against my better judgment.
I'll take a deep breath and drink the elixir that I've come to call Bittersweet Poetry.
It usually goes down smooth, but occasionally I choke on her bite.
I usually don't even notice when I finally let my insides out.

And so it begins…
My balance levels out with my state of mind,
Shaky at best.
Hands start drawing the pictures that I'm trying to get across,
As well as trying to read the situation because my sight's a bit blurry.
My words catch up to my thoughts, going a mile a minute,
Sometimes overshooting the exit and taking detours to get to the point.

Inner voices tell me to shut up and keep it together
When any other time they would say stop holding back.
That's why I wear my heart on my sleeve right above the word 'Break'
Sometimes I'll sharpie in '–ing' and other times '–er,'
And on my worst nights '–fast.'
On my best nights, I write 'Stopping' or 'Sealing' above my heart.

Either way, I'll wake up the next morning feeling like I had to stuff my insides back in through my ear.
Then, I'll check my call logs and receipts to dissipate or confirm fears.
Then, I sit back and reflect on if it was worth heckling Jekyll enough to let Hyde come and play.

Drunk Disclaimer

Allow me to welcome you
To the late show…
Quick disclaimer,
I knew it was a problem when three different people told me not to drink too much before performing.
My first thought was when was the last time I ever did that?…
Second of all, is it really that noticeable?

I figured if I was tripping, I could play it off like, "Giiirl, you got me falling for you already."
Act like it was a test for the one that I need to be there on my worse nights
Before seeing me at my best.
But my vision is not the best.
Like my message, it sometimes gets a little blurred
When I'm not quite sober…
Burely able to keep my eyes focused enough to make hi contact.

I don't always know how to hold my liquor, so I drink it.
Especially since the key to whisking you off your feet seems to be whiskey.
So shots are lined up for every hair on my chinny chin chin.
Chin up when ingesting cocktails for confidence.
It's fast acting as it burns all hesitation from my throat,
Before the chill hits my spine,
Pulling shoulders back,
Finally settling the butterflies in my gut.

Hey self, quick sidebar,
I think you're be(gin)ning to show signs of dependency.
And depending on how you look at it,
It's pretty funny how…
Wait, what was funny?...
Funny how family secrets only seem to hurt the family that they're kept from.
They found it relevant to tell me that one wasn't around because he was abusive,
While the other one wouldn't let anyone into his mind.
Mind you, he's the same one that they say I take after.
They told me that my grandpa was quiet, but quite contagious…courageous off of the same mixture that I call my drink of choice.
That would have been nice to know…

Would have been nice to know…
Before nightcaps became my handicap.
Before I put my heart on the top shelf,
A little too far back to see where exactly,
So it's a stretch any time I reach out emotionally.

A double dose on deck to relieve any strained affections,
Battling any infections brought on by rotted feelings and ink poisoning.
Because tainted love often leads to bad blood, where anything might be said
When I want to kill a potential for me to be vulnerable.
I'll explain away confessions as idle words
Fueled by vodka when feelings are clear to see, but still hard to swallow.

A grey goose carries messages, too heavy for a pigeon,
So that I can spend the nights lighthearted,
Knowing that the suspended weight will land on my head as soon as I open
my eyes the next day.
And now it's hello hangover.
It hasn't been long enough,
But I've been swerving around issues so long that it might be hard to see
what I'm driving at.
I'm not as sharp as I could be because I don't want to cut you deep enough to
leave scars,
So I dull myself enough to only scratch the surface
And blame any bad performance on or off the mic on the bartender
To bar any tender spots from being struck.
So without any further ado, welcome to my intoxicating point of view.

Bittersweet Poetry

We met on a night when I was feeling lonely and she looked mighty cold.
I thought that I didn't have anything to lose, so I put my hand around this southern belle,
Who recognized the gentleman in me and didn't pull away from my touch.
She whispered that she'd take me places that I'd never dream of, so I said let's go.

The next thing I knew, her tongue was halfway down my throat.
I gripped her frame a little tighter as we warmed to each other's touch.
She left my mouth numb and my knees weak,
But when I came up for air, I knew that we were just getting started.

She helped ease my mind after long days and got me comfortable stepping into the spotlight.
The same light was used in my interrogations on nights that started with her but ended with unexpected results.
I had off nights and forgot how to handle the glares when I shine.
Never knowing if I should say thank you or I'm sorry to those that flock to the light,
Some found comfort by the warmth while others were burned from getting too close.

Unfortunately, I wasn't immune to my own glow and that started the beginning of the end for us.
I felt unappreciated, like all of my good intentions and feelings were ending up wasted.
That's when her cousin gave me a shot to chase her, and though I knew that they didn't mix well,
I took it thinking that her intentions were see-through, but she was just trying to kill a bit of time.
I was caught up before I even left the building, though I didn't know how deep I was in.
She brought it up on the way home,
Making me swerve while trying to maintain control of the wheel.
She made it worse when I got stopped, by telling the officer that I had hit her earlier in the night.

It's bittersweet, but I had to leave her alone without a kiss goodbye
Because I know her kiss might draw me back in.
After a night of reflection and months apart, I finally saw her with someone else.

She called from her seat in VIP, saying that he didn't mean a thing and that she wanted me back,
But I've moved on and doing better without her.
Plus, it's nice not having to spend so much money for her company,
And I realized that I really needed to stop talking to my drinks.

A Sober Heart

"I love you, but I've chosen darkness"

Hearts Mend and Hearts Break

The world's worst feeling
Is to know you're right for them,
But they're wrong for you.

Match Made

We have been perfect for others,
But together
We can be broken.

The Lie For The Unknown
You want to know why
I lie when it matters most.
So I won't scare you.

Dangerous

I'm afraid of her.
She can make me a killer,
Protecting our love.

Mind My Heart

Love on my mind, but not in my heart.

I often have a good idea, but no desire to put it into action.

And once it finally finishes the transfer from my head to my chest,

I'm left wondering what I was thinking, with a full heart but no outlet for the love.

In The Shadow of Tears

I love you,
But I've chosen darkness.

In the dark, it's easier to get away with mistakes.
It can be blamed on the lack of vision.
No one can see your true intentions or emotions.
And if you're quiet enough, no one will know that you were even there.

Sometimes, I just feel like destroying something beautiful,
And I'd hate myself if that happened to be you.
Not that I would do it intentionally,
But I've been in the dark for so long
That my eyes might not adjust quick enough to realize it was you that I was
hurting.

My apology would be overshadowed by the regret that I knew better,
Insincere because I knew that I would do this,
But I was still too selfish to give you up.
Sentenced to seeing the brightness of your smile dimmed by my cloudy
judgment,
I'm left caught in the shadow of your tears.

From/To: Love – To/From: Hate

Because I've always loved her,

I hate what happened between us.

All because we agreed that we didn't want our reputation to be greater than the sum of its parts,

Things got out of hand once other perspectives broke in, and I came out the bad guy.

I tell her that she's the only one that gets all of me and that's the truth,

Though she's not the only one that's intrigued by me.

To those that don't know us, it appears like I've become what they expected me to be.

I just let them believe what they believe, so that my real goals can be realized unhindered.

I've been at this long enough to know how to handle the hazards, but still flirt with danger to keep things interesting.

I keep my distance because that's what good guys do and I don't want a morning of regrets.

Thanks to my friends' suggestions some nights run late, talking shop and relieving stress.

I soon get talked into proving that I'm as good as the rumors say

Only to be found surrounded by glass walls, quickly filling up with tears containing memories of fights, hurt feelings, and assumptions.

Bottle in hand, so that if drowning were to occur that it would at least taste good going down,

And then she left me.

Though she became the one jealous of all the attention that I get,

She kept saying that I was too sensitive and took things too personal.

She kept saying that I was too sensitive and took things too personal,

Though she became the one jealous of all the attention that I get.

And then she left me,

Bottle in hand, so that if drowning were to occur that it would at least taste good going down,

Only to be found surrounded by glass walls, quickly filling up with tears containing memories of fights, hurt feelings, and assumptions.

I soon get talked into proving that I'm as good as the rumors say.

Thanks to my friends' suggestions some nights run late, talking shop and relieving stress.

I keep my distance because that's what good guys do and I don't want a morning of regrets.

I've been at this long enough to know how to handle the hazards, but still flirt with danger to keep things interesting.

I just let them believe what they believe, so that my real goals can be realized unhindered.
To those that don't know us, it appears like I've become what they expected me to be.
Though she's not the only one that's intrigued by me,
I tell her that she's the only one that gets all of me and that's the truth.
Things got out of hand once other perspectives broke in, and I came out the bad guy,
All because we agreed that we didn't want our reputation to be greater than the sum of its parts.
I hate what happened between us
Because I've always loved her.

Tracks of Tears

They say that tears are the fuel that waters our growth,
What keeps our hearts from hardening due to bitterness,
And the proof that some people can still caress our cheeks with feelings.
No matter the distance in between us.

Initial Insight

These initials aren't for Stephen H. Sharpe.

SHS stands for Still Healing Slowly

Because I have a bad habit of picking at my scabs.

Honest Moment

I'm really not as even-keeled as I let on.
I could easily be labeled as an extreme case of polar opposites,
Showing signs of having the balance of a see-saw.
Sad face and hee-haw,
I love too deeply,
And sometimes don't care at all,
But will behave myself simply because I'd rather not deal with the fallout.

I'm the hero and the villain,
Prince Charming and Royal Pain,
Sympathizer and Womanizer,
Optimist and Pessimist,
Obsessive addict and indifferent observer,
A pillar of reason and empathy,
An emotional and malicious wreck.

So yes, her interest surprised me.
Why would she pick me?
You see, I want a girl when I want a girl.
And when I don't want a girl, I want a girl who understands that.
I appreciate the chase,
But I'm not trying to run a marathon before the marathon of love.
I'll drop out if it's drawn out too long, with no end in sight.

With a little insight, it's easy to see that for all my poetic gymnastics,
I'm awkward as hell in person.
More often than not, I'll second guess my way out of your interest and life.
But if you stick around, I'll tell you beautiful things to cushion my ugly.
I will never tell you a lie but might withhold the truth.
I'm quiet so that I can choose my words carefully,
But the arguments with myself can be deafening.
I'll let you in if you know the password,
Can answer one of my riddles,
Or prove interesting enough for me to venture out.
Though I must say, it's a jungle in here,
Not too many have escaped fully intact.

Because to know me is to hate me,
The overriding emotion in the complexity that is me.
You'll love me for the words that I say to lift your spirits,

But will be terrified of the expression that I have if you ever catch me when I think that I'm alone.
My revelry in my enigmatic nature will only draw your enmity,
Especially if I love you then leave you,
Only to fall back in love with you after realizing how special you are to have put up with me in the first place.
I am indeed,
A sad sight to see.
People hate what they don't understand.

And I hate not knowing if I'm worth loving or can ever fully be understood.
I don't know if I can call this is an honest moment
Or if it will be written off as another poem inspired by someone else's point of view.
Who knows…
Me?

I Wonder

I wonder...
I wonder...
I wonder a lot about myself,
But some of the questions only seem to come up when there's no one around
to provide an answer.

I wonder if she knows that she helped me to find my voice.
The voice that wanted to ask her to wait, but didn't want to seem selfish by
doing so.
I had hoped that she would just know and agree, but understand why she
didn't.
Because I didn't speak up and pass along what my heart was whispering.
A promise was made to never hold my tongue again or let my mouth get in
the way of nourishment for the soul.

I wonder if he tells her that she's beautiful,
Not with words but with looks from across the room,
Caresses her after a long day's work,
And gives flowers just because it's Wednesday.

I wonder if she knows that the pain of our separation made all subsequent
endings easier to bear,
Even with her who could have been the one but picked door number two.
Sometimes, I wonder how I can be so callous and so loving at the same time.

After asking me, "What's worse: unrequited love or having love that's
reciprocal but that you can't do anything about it?"
I wonder what went through her mind when she saw my hesitation.
I wonder why she told me what happened between her and her father a year
after it happened.
Was my anticipated reaction so scary that she waited so long?

So long I've wondered what people think of me,
And what they think my motivation is for the things that I do.
I wonder if my sanity is questioned because you have to watch out for the
quiet ones.
Does their thinking change when they find out that I was born in Oakland,
and split my time growing between Southside Richmond and Hillside
Vallejo?
How about when they learn that I went to a top 50 college and a top 25 grad
school based on academics?

The makings of a maniac,
A brainiac surrounded by tragedy,
I've been told that what doesn't kill you makes you stronger.
So I wonder how strong I must be to have carried my brother's coffin,
How smart I must be after a swollen brain,
How much love I have to give with my irregular heartbeats,
And how thick my skin and how powerful my voice must be after walking
off a slit throat.

Old blood shed for new family.
A brother from another mother,
A sister born to a different mister,
Kin related through past sins,
In-laws to similar crimes,
Welcome me back into the fold.

I wonder if they'll believe all or nothing that I say.
I wonder if any of them really know me.
I wonder…
I wonder…

Drunk Dialing

"You deserved my best…"

Drafts

I couldn't tell you
How many messages are
Drafts addressed to you.

I'm Sorry to Thank You
You...
You've been almost everything that I needed,
But all you've seen is me not be myself.
You held me down at my worst,
And encouraged me to live up to my potential.

You deserved my best,
But always got the leftovers.
You caught me on the rebound,
And I've been bouncing around ever since,
While you've been patiently waiting for me to make my move.

Where Do We Go From Here?

It's crazy to think about all that we've been through.
We succeeded where we should have failed,
And failed where we should have succeeded.
We found happiness and were rewarded for takings risks,
Though we did a lot of what we shouldn't have.

You probably shouldn't have given your number to a drunk,
Especially when that was how you ended your first conversation with him.
I shouldn't have started dating a coworker,
Knowing that people talk and how it could blow up in my face.
I knew that I shouldn't have let you go.
I just wanted you to be happy, and you said that you needed space to smile.
You shouldn't have come back
To face possible rejection and scarred feelings.
We shouldn't have pushed each other away
When we needed to hold on tighter than ever.
We shouldn't have let frustrations influence how we treated each other.
Every time one of us took something to heart that should've been forgotten,
We shouldn't have let it sink in and poison our well.
Who could've dreamed that we'd beat so many odds only to throw in the
towel over thinly spread feelings?

We shouldn't have been a couple.
But we were.
And we were amazing.
We cut out the joy to avoid the pain,
But we shouldn't have.
So I keep asking myself,
Where do we go from here?

Confession of a Broken Heart

I may never answer your call,
Will always hold some ill will
For the way you made me feel,
But I won't ever lose sight of what I learned.

Through all of the tough memories,
I appreciate the growth that you nurtured
That led to me speaking up and out,
The technique to ease my allergies,
And the theory of filling holes in our lives.

Through your abuse of the phrase
"In God we trust,"
You taught me that age is no indicator of maturity.
Thank you for showing me my maturity
And capacity to love and to stand by my standards.
I hope that you learned something too,
And that both our hearts do better.

Passing Thoughts

You've been dead to me ever since you broke my heart and ran away with
another man.
But finding out that you were dead to everyone else still came as a shock.
Though I welled up a bit when people shared stories of you,
The dam of tears never broke.
I didn't spill a single drop.
It was still damn you for what you did to me.

For a while, I hoped that you were miserable,
That you regretted leaving,
That the grass was moldy and muddy on the other side,
That you finally realized that those snakes in sheepskin whispering words of
advice were really poisoning your thoughts.

But distance brings perspective,
So I wished you well because I know that you were good for me.
You helped me to grow and to learn about myself,
What I wanted, and what I could handle.

I found myself with a shorter temper than usual, weeks after I got the news.
I was flashing on things that I knew weren't worth the energy.
I knew why when I almost destroyed something that you gave me,
So I focused my energy on checking up on our mutual friends.

Some reached out to me first,
We shared info and memories.
Others were surprised to hear from me.
I could tell that they didn't know what to say.

I finally accepted that I was mad that I knew you'd probably still be alive,
If only you had stayed here.
Though we didn't leave on good terms,
I'd never deny that you made a positive impact on me.
May you rest in peace while I sift through the rest of my pieces.

Blossom
I hope that you become as memorable as forget-me-nots,
As synonymous with love as a rose,
As grounded and strong as the roots of a fig tree,
With a smile as bright as a sunflower,
With dreams that reach higher than a redwood.
Keep blossoming.

A Letter for Kylee
Hey Lil Lady,

I was having a rough day, so I thought that I'd write to you.
No matter what I'm going through, just the thought of you picks my spirit up.
I miss you,
More than you'd ever believe.
I don't know the next time that I'll be able to see you,
But I want you to know that Daddy loves you.

I'm told that energy is never created or destroyed,
So even though you haven't been born yet
I know that you exist out there somewhere.
The late night jolts from being kicked in my bed,
Only to wake up tangled in the sheets alone.
The baby nudges to start looking for a bigger living space and a safer car to drive,
Which I credit to just wanting to be more "grown."

I'm sorry that it's taking me so long to hold you,
But it's my job to make your life as great as possible.
If I rush things for my own selfish reasons,
It'll end up hurting both of us.
After seeing friends who are only able to see their children on weekends or after cross-country trips,
I've doubled my efforts to be able to wake up and watch you sleep in the middle of any given night.
I refuse to fight with your mom and going our separate ways,
Only to be reminded of her smile every time you look up at me.

It's getting harder to keep going on,
Though each one hurts less,
I still feel like I'm running out of gas.
Fighting the urge to settle because I want the best for you,
I don't mind sacrificing easy days to keep smiles on your face.
So here's to looking at you kid,
Daddy loves you.

Sonrise

My son,

I hope that you look enough like me to know who's your daddy
But different enough to be your own man.
You won't fully understand what that means until you're older.

I hope that you're not as curious as I am,
That you'll see no need to explore how much trouble trouble really is.
I hope that you quickly learn how to leave well enough alone
And know well enough when you shouldn't be alone.
Don't be afraid to be alone,
But don't let yourself get lonely.

I hope that you're not shy,
That you'll talk to everyone that you exchange glances or smiles with.
Know your strengths and weaknesses
And how people can take advantage of both.

It'll help you find the one who will make you want to work harder and do better
Without even having to say anything.
She should be the one who will stick with you even after the arguments
And will get upset if anyone else tries to butt in or say something bad about you.
Don't be so worried about her feelings that you don't express yours.
It's better to have to explain things
Than to have her thinking that you don't care enough to make the effort.

All this is for you to understand where I've been and who I was.
You inherit my legacy.
I want to give you what's priceless:
A legacy of curiosity, integrity, kindness,
Love, and encouragement.

Never be afraid to challenge yourself or the world around you.
Leave no question unasked
And no feelings unexpressed.
Never forget that I'll always love you.
Never forget that I'll always love you.
Just remember that I planted the seed,
And I will weed out any thorns in my side.

The Last Party
Dear Mr. Robert Downey Jr.,

I wanted to take the time to express how great of an actor you are,
And how much I appreciate your work as well as what you've been through.
I can relate to your story and wanted to extend an invitation to one last party.

Like you, I've been in the public eye from a young age,
And I was also named after my dad.
You were probably teased because of it.
Always called the number 2, or the second coming,
Probably called a downer being Mr. RD and all because everyone wants to hit the road.
I was told that I wasn't the sharpest tool in the shed,
Though they were the ones who could never get my name right on the first try.
I learned to shed thin skin,
And to embrace being the soloist.

I became the quiet guy that made people laugh to remember to keep a smile on his own face.
I was called Charlie Cheerful, but felt like a bum.
I put on a suit of armor to face the world,
But I still can't face myself.

Like you, I studied methods of playing a part,
Engrossed myself in the storm until I could predict the thunder
By analyzing the world around me down to the smallest tipping point.
Basically, I made a career of being someone else,
By creating a poker face for my poker face.

Now, people don't really get me until they study my zodiac,
And then it all clicks.
Hopefully, they recognize it before getting cut on sharp tongues.
It runs in the family,
Like the twitch of an alcoholic's bite
On that familiar taste of gunmetal.
I can relate to the moments where it seems hard to breathe,
Choking on words, with only laughs to greet the grave nature of explaining situations.

We celebrated the good times by getting into bad situations.

We drank to have an excuse for behavior
That's always lurking beneath the surface.
Thoughts often alternate between urges to kiss kiss and other times bang
bang,
Accompanied by that chill that you get when feelings ice over while the
blood heats up,
Along with a tingle that works it way down to the fingertips.
Hands often move without a purpose or purposely held at bay away from
stirring up bad intentions.
I scan the dark for familiar sights,
And I might hone in on the usual spots.

I leave each time, promising that this was the last party,
But who knows if that's true?
Because I'd do anything to keep from feeling less than zero.
I just hope that it'll be better tomorrow.
If you're anything like me,
You never need to worry during the day so I wish you
Good night and good luck.

Sincerely,

Stephen Sharpe

Drunk Confessions

"…my smile is more muscle memory than emotion."

Dedication

This is for me,
So that I'll never forget what I've been through,
And to leave a map of where my mind has roamed.

This is for my wife,
So that she'll know what she's getting herself into,
And as a thank you for being my ultimate muse.

This is for my children,
So that they'll know that I never had it all together,
And as warning and encouragement to do better.

This is for the strangers,
So that they'll have a story to pass the time,
And to let them know that they are not alone.

Autophobia

I write because I'm afraid that I'll leave too soon,
That I won't get to say goodbye,
That I won't get to explain myself,
Or that I'll forget everything that's important to me.

So I write it all down,
All the memories,
Stories, emotions,
And who inspired them all.
I'm afraid of misunderstandings, forgetting, and things left unsaid.

Between These Lips

Sometimes the ego
Of my top lip fights the heart
Of my lower lip.

Johnny Depth

It started when I young.
They always said that I was different but never gave the same reason how:
It was my curiosity, my ability to see the world through rose-colored shades,
Being able to adapt no matter the situation, able to relate to other's feelings,
or my intelligence.
I just took it with fear and loathing that I saw the world differently than those
my own age.
I was able to fully comprehend the nightmare that's at the helm of these
streets.
While everyone else around me embraced it, I just watched through my
secret window.

They called me Edward Scissorhands because I seemed a little off and kept
my hands to myself.
It's true that I'm a little off, but I've always been known for my precision.
Early on, I learned the subtle methods of how to cut layers off in different
ways,
And that left me dangerous like Dillinger,
Too smart for my own good and only getting caught if I got sloppy.
As I got older, the nickname stuck but I didn't want to sound strange,
So I changed my last name to Sharpe.

These days, people want to know what's eating me,
Not realizing that I'm still mad as a hatter with my head in the clouds,
I'm trying to find Neverland,
Hoping to meet the astronaut's wife, and that she can help me reach that
happily ever after.
But that seems less and less likely after that time in Mexico,
Where I almost got caught up when my eye was on a sparrow,
Whose eyes can only be recalled with a bottle of rum.
After a while, I outgrew the taste that had become too sweet,
So I was recommended whiskey so I can grow some whiskers and avoid
being called a babyface.
Over the years, I've learned how to play many different roles, but seem to be
typecast all the same.
I do it better than most, so I guess that's why they call me Johnny Depth at
the end of the day.

Point of View

If I took you to the top of Mount Ego,
We would just barely see over the ridge
Of the Valley of My Insecurities.

Muted

Sometimes I hide all of my pens,
Shut down my laptop,
And lock my phone,
All to keep from writing.

The throbbing in the back of my arm,
Just about the elbow,
Makes my fingers numb.
A storm of thoughts beat against my eardrums.
Paranoia pokes at my lungs and stomach trying to make me spill my guts.
Worries try to misdirect my eyes to slight my hand.

Sometimes the darkness sees me at my most honest,
With silence being my best confidant.
I've learned that some things are better left marinating in the unsaid.

The Punch Line
Sigh Another long day is ahead of me.
Alone in my room, but it's not quite time to get ready.
Another sleepless night has me brooding in my chair,
As I sit here watching my mask continue to stare.
Stare at me with that blank look, with its painted-on smile,
Taunting me as I contemplate for a while.

How did I get to where I'm currently at?
I followed my dream, and my dad's book helped me with that.
All I ever wanted to do was to make people happy
And that brought me to sitting in this chair, sadly.
I slowly paint a portrait of myself.
Though crooked and blurry, it's better than anyone else.

I thought that I'd be happy living life as a clown.
Little did I know, it's harder than it sounds.
Something so scary to more than a few,
At first I didn't know why, but now I have a clue.
How can someone be smiling and cheerful all of the time?
I know now what goes on in a clown's mind.

Always performing and trying to come up with new jokes,
But what happens when they hear, "That's all folks?"
They leave with no care of what happens to you next.
But at the next show, I already know what they expect.
They want to laugh and cheer and see you do silly things,
Not caring about a clown's tears or the lonely song that he sings.
Why would they? It's all a part of the show.
Even his tears are painted on, didn't you know?

A clown doesn't cry, worry, or ever get depressed.
He's never heartbroken or looks like he needs more rest.
I know my job, and they say I do it well.
Never off the mark, and when I am you couldn't tell.
They say, 'Oh, don't worry. He has something up his sleeve.'
And who am I to disappoint? I aim to please.
So I play the part until the end of the day,
But then that's only the start of my day.

So here I am, sitting alone trying to come up with new material.
They say, 'Life's a big joke so why be so serial?'

…Wait, what am I saying? I meant serious.
Wow, great, now I'm sounding delirious.
Scratch that joke and put it with the rest.
I've played my part, but still not my best.
I still can't find that one joke that will last,
Maybe it's because I don't know what makes a clown laugh.

Lockdown

Some poems aren't meant to be read.
Some are paper prisons meant to hold delinquent and undesirable thoughts and ideas,
And reading them might instigate the next prison riot.

Poets Anonymous

Hi,
My name is Stephen,
And I'm an addict.
In my worst times, I was hitting it two to three times a day.
The longest I've been clean in the last 17 years is eight or nine months.

I've written 628 poems,
273 are about love,
And 189 of them try to explain myself to myself and others.
I've had seven muses,
Countless dealers,
Accidentally fumbled and broken four hearts that I'm aware of,
And scared more than a few people who thought that they could stomach a tour behind the scenes.

I'm not one to share pens with just anybody.
I don't know where theirs have been.
I haven't edited enough to seem sufficiently clean to entertain company.
Plus, I worry that my things will go missing if I share too much.

I've tried group therapy,
But hearing other people's stories usually drives me to try new strains
And spiral deeper into the lines cut with ink.
The itch always starts in my right arm,
Creeps up my spine,
And consumes my thoughts until I satisfy my urge.
Almost anything can spark it.
But when I see someone else using,
I know it's only a matter of time until I'm at it again.

I've smoked through notebooks,
Rolled receipts and napkins,
Tapped phones and computers,
And scrawled ink on my skin when there's nothing else within reach.
Never caring who's watching,
I've done it in cars, trains, coffee houses, lounges, bars,
Weddings, funerals, and too many other places to remember.
I'm at my worst when I'm alone,
Roaming through rooms and streets talking to myself.
Looking for a quick fix with a haiku
Or an epic that'll take days or even weeks to get out of my system.

120

I like the highs,
And even the lows don't seem that bad on most days.
So I can't see myself trying sobriety
Because I don't think I really have a poetry problem.

Boredom

Boredom is a hell of a thing.

I've gotten into too many arguments and relationships simply to fill time and make things interesting.

Just because I had nothing better to do.

Just to explore something new.

I usually never come back to my boredom's solution once it's done its job.

Unfortunately or fortunately.

Another Story
Every night is another story,
Another excuse,
Another lie,
Another time that I'm almost glad to wake up with memory gaps.

Another night spent where you, me, and the bottle makes three.
I really need to stop talking to my reflection.
We always argue about the past, present, and future,
Discuss how my execution is bad, but my intentions are good,
And about how we keep stepping on each other's toes.

We agree to be better people,
To be more considerate,
And to part ways with each other.
But that's another story
That none of us believe.

Know When to Fold

I have a habit of holding onto things for too long.
I'll rock it until the wheels fall off,
Then will teach myself how to ride a unicycle.
I balance faults and justifications like lady justice.
And we all know that she favors the perpetrator,
If I play my cards right.

Not Worth It

Let me let you go before it's too late.
I'll love you always and never.
I'll keep you falling in love with me,
And hating me for doing it.
I'm not worth your feelings.

The Art of Love
I've origami'd many hearts into poems,
And often turn my pain into paper cranes.

Looking for Trouble

I'm learning how to better read the universe.
When I try to line up excuses for being out or justify questionable decisions,
They tend to fall apart before I even leave the house.

I'm starting to realize that some things aren't worth fighting for,
That some distractions can lead to longer detours than intended,
That sometimes it's best to sit still and wait things out.

I remind myself to not forget the destination worrying too much about the path,
To stop second guessing gut feelings,
That patience is better than curiosity,
And that I value virtue over vindication.

Love Jones

You weren't supposed to fall for him.
I tried to keep you two apart,
But he has a smoother approach and an answer for everything.

I know what comes next.
He'll never say that he wants you and only you,
But he won't be afraid to tell you that he's more man than most.
He'll do all the things that you let him,
Yet won't make you feel bad for holding back.

You were looking for happiness,
While he'll settle for a little inspiration.
He remembers faces and places but never names or shames.

The mystery of his appeal is that he's an oxymoron.
He claims to be looking for an intellectual equal,
But will bide time with foxy morons.
I've seen him fool people by telling the truth,
Shame others with their own words,
And twist wills like steel with a magnetic charm.

I've watched poems and conversations conducted as experiments
To prove theories on affecting emotions and motivations without expressing commitment.
I told him to watch his step,
And that I know why he doesn't dance.
It's because his rhythm doesn't match the beat of the questions
That he's used to two-stepping around.

Questions like why would anyone start conversations with wallflowers just to ease loneliness?
It's to get a closer look at their petals,
Caressed by hands that have been softened by too many tears.
Some of them have fallen for me,
Others for him,
And in the worse cases for both of us.
But they all still blame me.

I'm sorry.
I sometimes refer to myself in third person to try to distance myself,
Turning my history into his story.

128

A quiet guy who's broken out of his shell
But damaged nerves in the process.
Now, my smile is more muscle memory than emotion.
I'll touch feelings without attachments.
I'm not good at staying away from old wounds.
I'll make you appreciate the little things like he does,
That's how I stretch the good,
So that the shortcomings don't seem as bad.
I just wish that your mothers told you never to fall for a Love Jones.

Some Days
Some days I don't recognize myself.

To Do List

Fix the sheets. I can't tell if the bed was hit by a tornado, a nightmare, or a passionate lover.

Fix the lamp. Just because it's dark, doesn't mean that you have an excuse to break things.

Fix the chair. It's still wobbly and you shouldn't have to be cautious when you're trying to relax.

Fix the toilet. You can't flush away all of the evidence of what happened.

Fix the hinges. The door cries every time you leave and yells when you come back.

Fix the intake valve. Whiskey is not a sustainable fuel source and is bad for the environment.

Fix the answering machine. You know that you won't call them back anytime soon.

Fix your sleep patterns. In bed by 2:00 AM and up again at 6:00 AM is no way to spend your nights.

Fix your fingers. They crack and pop on their own from holding on to things too tightly and for too long.

Fix your shoulder. Carrying their problems for so long has them forgetting that they left things with you and that you have your own baggage to handle.

Fix your handkerchief. You keep using it to clean the messes made by the pins sticking a heart.

Fix your lips. They filter what should be said far too often and then overcompensate with ramblings.

Fix your glasses. You keep seeing connections where there aren't any and go down the wrong paths.

Fix your to do list. A lot of these things have been on the list for too long.

The Replay

I really can't count
The times that I've second guessed
The second guesses.

Lost Language

I wish that I still knew sign language,
So that I could point out all the things
That I don't know how to say.

134

Advice Anonymous

"Stop breathing new life into old pain."

Who Told You?

While walking in this jungle that we call Earth,
Many will try to poke holes in the fabric of others' self-worth
To patchwork their own lives.
So I ask, who told you that you were flawed?
Who told you that you were lacking something?

Who told you that your curls needed to be straight?
Was it the ones that don't naturally have them?
The same ones who produce products that straightens your hair by
weakening it,
Slowly losing its shine and ability to hold itself together, breaking locks,
Leaving it brittle and continuously shedding its former beauty?

Who told you that you weren't the right size?
As long as you're not so heavy to make light of your health
Or too frail to stand strong in a storm,
You are a walking work of art.
Each stretch mark tells a story.
The ones on your thighs grew from carrying the weight of the world,
Yet you still stand strong.
And what about the ones along your side reminding you of when you first
learned to cook for yourself and others?

Who told you that you needed to wrap your frame in designer clothes?
It often costs the same to make as the lesser known brands,
But with the right seal of approval...I mean logo, companies can charge
more.
They're often worn by those needing validation by wearing the same things
as celebrities.
And what is a celebrity?
People behaving crazily, and some celebrate it, why?
Because of their "freedom to express themeselves?"
Because of that, I sometimes shed a tear.

Who told you that men can't cry?
Was it the ones who say that tears are a sign of weakness?
It sometimes takes more strength to let them fall than to bottle them up.
Don't let the pressure build up, only for it to then flare out of control
Onto whoever might be too close for comfort but too far for understanding.

I don't understand those hating on my honey graham cracker, caramel complexion.
Who told you that your chocolate skin isn't gorgeous?
Was it the ones who tan to bridge the gap between our tones?
The same ones whose skin isn't as tested as yours?
You are full of melanin, looked at by society as a possible felon in waiting,
When in reality, like a melon in waiting, you're ripe with potential.

Who told you that you aren't smart?
Was it the ones who have $200,000 receipts…I mean degrees that say that they are?
Some have graduated school but still haven't learned their lessons.
Who told you that you were less because you've been through more?
Don't you know that even diamonds have flaws and are made through almost unbearable pressures?

Who dared to tell you that you couldn't make your dreams come true?
You'll never know your capacity unless you're willing to test your limits,
Learn from mistakes, and not be afraid of the unknown.

Who made you ashamed of what you don't have instead of proud of your gifts and experiences?
Did you eat that fruit that looked good but turned out to be rotten?
Has it made you always second guess trying to take a bite of something new?
Weren't you created pure, born beautiful, cut from the fabric of holy origins,
Essentially set apart by your uniqueness?

Who told you that no one cared or would ever love you?
Does everyone have the same eye color?
Do all grow to be the same height?
No matter how overwhelming the majority may seem,
People are not all the same,
The right ones just haven't found you yet.
Just don't hide or stay silent when they come looking.

Sticks & Stones

Sticks and stones may break my bones, but words will never leave me.
Words can hurt when they're used against me once or done repeatedly.
The worst part about words is that you can never see them coming,
So I can't guard against them or stop the verbal thumping.
Even if I close my ears and eyes,
I'll feel them eventually, leaving deeper impressions than any stick snapped
or stone crumpled on my mind.

Words never leave a mark, so you won't see these wounds of mine.
You wouldn't know that it's too soon for me to be patted on my spine.
I know you mean well but the touch will only hurt me more.
Like internal bleeding or having just gone 12 rounds with life, I'm feeling
more than a little bit sore.
Sticks and stones may break my bones, but the hurt depends on how hard you
heave them.
That's why words are worse because though they might hurt, they're that
much worse if I believe them.

Conscientious

Dear Friend,

Please be responsible with your words.
Please be responsible for your words.

Though you sometimes use could've/should've/would've beens to patchwork
tattered memories,
Be careful choosing the shades used to paint your inspiration.
You say that they'll never see or hear it once it's finished,
Yet put it on full display,
Yet you tell me not to worry because it's framed in a way to hide identities.

But what if they did see it?
What if they do recognize all your familiar tendencies?
Would they be proud to have been your muse?
Would it make them see their errors and any ways to become a better person?
Or would it make things worse?
Does your portrait embody them as they are or as they were?
Does it tear them down to the level that you've painfully pulled yourself up
from?

You might be right.
I could just be overthinking things.
After all, they're only words…
But correct if I'm wrong,
In some instances, isn't God Himself called the Word?
Living and powerful,
Sharper than any two-edged sword,
Piercing even to the division of soul and spirit,
Joints and marrow?

Yes, my friend,
Words can cut deep.
We've been hurt so much and it's taken so long to heal
That it's no wonder that we're experts at opening old wounds,
Scribing new scars into flesh,
And crumbling others' confidence from the inside out.

Like Frankenstein, we'll put pieces together,
Giving life to the wretched.
It's hard to look away

Because we package it with just enough lust and disgust
That people can't help but to rush to see something memorable.
But they will keep their distance to avoid the risk of getting ripped to shreds.

So what's your endgame?
Would you rather be a speaker for the dead and dying
Or a speaker for the lost?
Give voice to those who have lost smiles,
Lost love, lost relationships,
Lost a sense of self, lost motivation, or lost hope.
Be a beacon for those who've become lost in transition,
Lost in the motions, and lost in the commotion.

Do it because you were once lost,
And sometimes you still wander off the path.
Leave a guide to growth for yourself and others,
Just don't do it at the expense of another.
Say what should be said,
And vent in a vacuum when your growth will wither those around you.
You have a responsibility,
Not just at as writer but as a person.

Sincerely,

Your Conscience

Scars and Scabs

We all carry scars and scabs,
From falls, burns, and other mishaps.
Luckily, there are some that you can't see,
Those that come from words, thoughts, and other hidden edges.

At first impressions, I try to remember to not introduce the paranoia about my ears being too big,
The haircut that is not quite even, or any other imperfections that we pick at in the mirrors.
I can shake hands without worrying about their condition,
Some crippled from second guessing ever reaching out to someone or picking up a new endeavor.
Long sleeves aren't needed to cover how many times that we've tried to cut lives short with drugs and alcohol,
And I can wear shorts because my legs don't show the third degree burns from all of the lies from when I said that I'm fine.

I don't have to avert my eyes from seeing hearts that are bent out of shape,
Some smashed from crescent-shaped hands that became clenched fists.
While other hearts have been torn out and replaced so many times
That I can't even look down because they're dripping between our shoes.

Each day, I see more and more veterans from this war that we call life.
If we could see a little more of each other's scars and scabs,
I think that people would be a little more thoughtful and understanding.

Love & Happiness
Loving someone and
That mate making you happy
Are two different things.

Playing Chess

Living is like chess,
Sometimes you sacrifice pawns
That could have been queens.

Left Alone
Sometimes progress and innovation
Come from love loss and isolation.

Bone to Pick

Stop being so nice to them.
When they want to dig up the past,
Stop snatching the shovel to dig up the dead bodies.
Stop reviving old feelings.
Stop breathing new life into old pain.
Don't let dead relationships eat at your brain.
Let the dead remain where they lay.
That will let you rest in peace.

On The Edge
Some will cut you off,
Sprint away holding scissors,
Then ask for band-aids.

A Little Advice

Hey boss, I'm not tryna beg, but can ya spare a little bit?
I just need enough for a penny for your thoughts and to share my two cents.
I might not look like much now, but back in the day I was really something.
So I probably know you better than most people cuz there's nothing
That you can do to hide what's obvious to me.
I just wanna give ya a little advice if ya let me.

I know that look; you're not having the best of days.
You got that telescope look, eyes right here but your head's miles away.
You're walking a split second too slow, second-guessing everything that you do now.
You're far from happy and it shows in that smile, that's as fake as a clown's.
But you hold it firmly in place because you don't want to lose it like you lost your sense of direction,
No longer knowing which way to go, just coasting, hoping that one day it'll come to your recollection.
You're probably thinking, 'How does he know all of this?'
I'll let you in on a little secret...I'm a little bit psychic.
Oh, and it does help that we can always find our own.
I've been down that road before, and as a guide have made it my home.

I have a good eye for seeing those who've been where I've been and shared similar pain.
I just have one question to ask you... can you stand the rain?
Though it's probably the last thing on your mind right now, everybody has rainy days.
Whether it be from betrayal, losing someone close, not knowing yourself or if you'll make it through the day,
Broken hearts, not knowing when the next hit will come,
Or dependency on something that you used to do just for fun.
Yeah, I've seen it all and have done most of it too.
Whatever your struggle is, what are you going to let it do to you?
Change you? Sharpen you? Inspire you? Be the beginning of your end?
Rainy days can give you whatever you want out of them.

Like knowing when to carry an umbrella, it can be something you learn from,
The start of something new, like a garden of thorns before the first rose of spring has sprung,
That last straw, before you let the tears hidden in the downpour carry you away,

148

Or even that memory that never leaves you, that first kiss to warm you while standing in the rain.

But let me tell ya something, don't let the world get you down.
That's one of the few sayings that are true, though I know how cliché that sounds.
Don't let the world change ya because you've changed the world simply by your existence.
Without you, there would be a void that could never be filled. For instance, If someone else did what you do, then they couldn't do what they do now And the chain reaction goes on. What you fail to see is that you're that butterfly that's still crawling on the ground.
Your story is still being spun around you, your shell not yet hard enough to keep you from feeling others trying to interrupt your dreaming.
You're still learning how to be a thicker book than most people have time to spend reading.
Once you do that, you can fly above it all and only be touched by those worthy of your presence.
And that's just a little free advice from a stranger, so I was wondering if you could spare a few cents.

We Spring, Only to Fall
Leaves fall.
Rain falls.
So why do we think that we don't have to fall apart to grow?
Can the occasional fall be good for us?

What's Changed?
I stopped feeling sorry for us.

Keep Believing
Don't lose hope in love.
Don't you ever, dare lose hope in love.
That hope is the one thing that can never be taken away from you.

It will only be lost if you give up.
People can disappoint you, fail you, hurt you,
But they can also surprise you, strengthen you, and help you heal.

Hope is knowing who you are inside and out,
What you're capable of,
And trusting that God and the universe knows it too and will respond in kind.